This book belongs to
E. L. S. Ward
and is on loan to the
Wessex Guild of Bookbinders.

Please do not remove it from the bindery.

Introducing Bookbinding

Introducing Bookbinding

Ivor Robinson

B T Batsford Limited London
Watson-Guptill Publications New York

© Ivor Robinson 1968
Photographs by Ian Ross

First published 1968
Library of Congress Catalog Card Number 68-18706

Printed and bound in Great Britain by
Jarrold & Sons Ltd, Norwich
for the Publishers
B T Batsford Limited
4 Fitzhardinge Street London W1 and
Watson-Guptill Publications
165 West 46th Street New York NY 10036

Contents

Acknowledgment

The author wishes to thank the Principal of the Oxford College of Technology and the Head of its School of Design, for permission to photograph equipment within the bookbinding department of the college and to show examples of the work of its students.

Introduction

Bookbinding is an artistic craft of great antiquity, and at the same time, a highly mechanised modern industry. The division between craft and industry is not so wide, however, as might at first be imagined. Indeed, it is interesting to observe that the three main problems presented to the mass-production bookbinder of today, with his automated lines of machinery, are those that confronted the medieval craftsman. The first problem is still how to hold together the leaves of a book; the second, how to protect those leaves once they are held together; and the third, how to identify and/or decorate the protective cover.

These three problems are as fundamental now as they were during the early centuries of the craft. They are normally solved by a careful analysis of all the variables. Thus, consideration of the size of book, thickness of book, type of paper or other text material and its make-up, value of the text, particular requirements related to use, the expected life span of the book, the number of books to be bound and factors concerned with the economics of the total binding task.

The purpose of this present work is to offer an introduction to tools, equipment and materials of the craft together with sequential demonstration of basic bookbinding skills likely to be within the scope of an average school, college or similar miscellaneous hand bindery.

Oxford 1968   I.R.

9

Glossary

Forwarding the binding of a book up to the stage of lettering and decoration.

Finishing the lettering and decoration of a book.

Section the basic component of the body of a book, formed by folding a sheet of plain or printed paper into its subdivisions.

Leaf a single piece of paper hinging at the binding edge, usually formed when book edges are cut and the section folds or bolts are removed.

Page one side of a leaf, either recto or verso.

Back the binding edge of a book.

Back-edge those parts of sections, leaves and boards presented to the binding edge.

Foredge (fore-edge) the edge of leaves and boards opposite to the back-edge.

Head the top edge of leaves and boards.

Tail the bottom edge of leaves and boards.

Endpaper leaves variously formed and constructed which protect the first and last sections and provide an inner link between the body of a book and its boards.

Front board the board which protects the beginning of a book.

Off board the board which protects the end of a book.

Square that part of a board which extends beyond and protects the edges of a book.

Spine that part of the cover of a book which protects the back.

Joint the point of hinge between the body of a book, its boards and its spine.

Case the cover of a book made separately from its body and joined to the latter as a final operation, as opposed to traditional binding in which the boards are attached to the body before the covering material is applied.

The bindery

Bookbinding can best be carried out in a room with good even light, and a water source, sink and washing facilities in the room or nearby.

A bench of about 72×30 inches provides a minimum working area for one person. The bench height should be approximately 36 inches, thus allowing certain operations to be performed standing. A stool is required for operations carried out at the bench in a seated position. An additional bench or table is useful on which to place work awaiting attention, or in progress and between operations. Bench tops are ideally surfaced with linoleum so that they can easily be kept clean. Work benches and tables should be shielded from direct fierce sunshine. Gas or electricity points are needed for the heating of hot glues and finishing stoves.

The arrangement of benches, tables and equipment should be as logical as possible and give the craftsman the best use of available light and space, together with comfort when working and moving about the bindery.

Tools and equipment

A significant amount of bookbinding can be achieved with relatively little plant. A small number of basic items are desirable and these can be added to as skills, needs or ambitions develop. A comprehensive range of tools and equipment for bookbinding is shown here and in appropriate places throughout this book.

1 Tenon-saw, dividers, backing-hammer, spoke-shave, G-clamp, set-square, carpenter's square, various bone-folders, boxwood ruler, steel ruler

2 Oil-stone, leather strop, pair of shears, pair of scissors, 'French' paring-knife, 'German' paring-knife, penknife, shoe-maker's knife, card-knife, steel straight-edge

 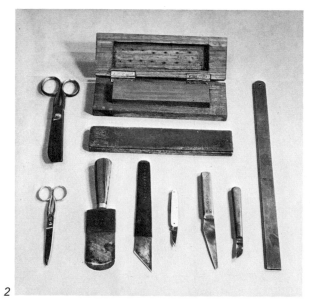

1   *2*

3 Paste-tub, glue-pot, polythene container for cold adhesives, a range of brushes, sponge

4 *Back* nipping-press on wooden stand, *left* cutting-press (i.e. lying-press with runners for plough) together with, plough and press-pin, *right* large lying-press, *front* small and large finishing or bench presses

4

3

5 *Back left* pressing-boards, *back right* metal-edged pressing-boards, *front* knocking-down iron, lead weights, cutting-boards, metal-edged backing-boards, backing-boards, smoothing-plane (for re-aligning backing-board bevel)

6 Finishing tools: *back* fillet and roll, *centre* handle-letters, type-holder with type, decorative tools, gouge, pallet, *front* two blocks

7 Sewing-frame, on which rest reels of tape and webbing together with thread in packet, unwrapped, in skein, and with skeins cut and plaited (appendix 1). In the foreground is a bodkin, sewing-keys for use with tape, needles, sewing-keys for use with cord (shown here for comparison only), a ball of hemp cord

5

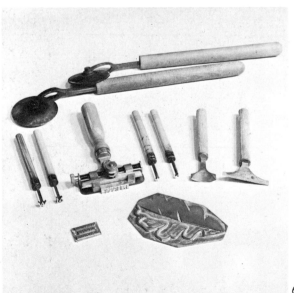

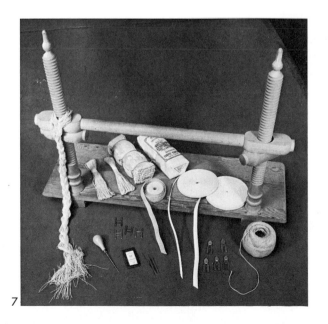

6 7

Materials and adhesives

The following lists of materials and adhesives are likely to be of use in general bookbinding operations.

White cartridge paper, white bank paper, white newsprint, brown kraft paper, coloured Ingres paper, coloured Cobb paper, decorative printed and marbled papers, coloured cover papers.
Strawboard, millboard.
Niger morocco goatskin, bookcloth and buckram woven covering-materials, white cotton label-cloth, mull (all shown in figure 8).
Fibre-felt (tough paper) covering-materials.
Scotch, flexible and case-making hot glues, polyvinyl-acetate (P.V.A.) general purpose cold glue, wheat-flour paste (appendix 2).
Gold leaf; gold, aluminium and pigment blocking foils.
Glaire (egg-albumen mordant), gold-rubber, vinegar, white Vaseline, cotton-wool, benzine, poster-colours, printing-inks.

8

15

Machine-direction in paper and boards

Most of the paper and board used in bookbinding and book production is machine-made. It is a feature inherent in machine manufacture that the cellulose-fibres from which the paper or board is made tend to be drawn into one general direction. This general fibre direction is called the grain or machine-direction.

Paper and boards bend more easily along their machine-direction than across. When made wet (e.g. with adhesive) paper stretches considerably more across than along its machine-direction and shrinks back when drying out.

In order to give greater ease in the opening of its leaves, greater rigidity and stability of its boards, elimination of creasing in endpaper paste-downs and elimination of the possibility of warping covers, the machine-direction in all the materials of a book should as a general rule run from head to tail. One possible exception may be made when selecting

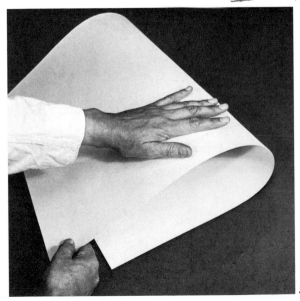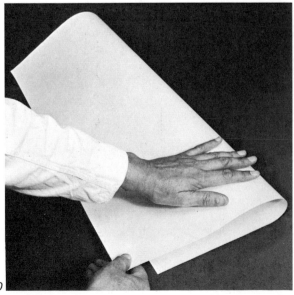

9   10

boards for oblong or landscape format books, but care must be taken when binding such to keep the moisture content of the adhesives used to a minimum, thus avoiding contrary shrinking of the various materials and subsequent warping.

Testing for machine-direction

9–10 The bend test to determine machine-direction in paper. Paper bends more easily along its machine-direction than across

11 The tear test to determine machine-direction in paper. A straighter tear is obtained with rather than against the machine-direction

12 The wet test to determine machine-direction in paper. The strips of paper have been sponged with water. The direction along the tunnel of paper indicates the machine-direction

13 Bending a strawboard to determine its machine-direction

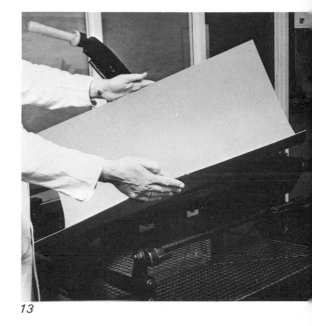
13

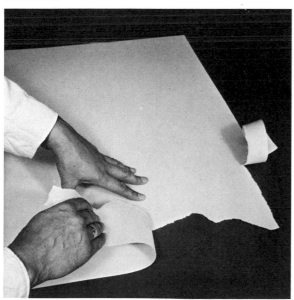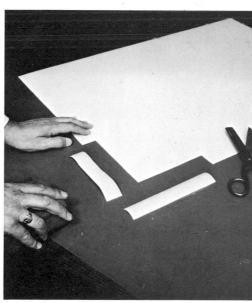
11 12

17

The make-up of books and folding from sheets

14 Most books begin their lives as flat printed sheets. The ultimate format of a book depends upon the size of the sheet and the way in which the printer has set out or imposed his pages of type-matter or illustration. Sheets are based on standard broadsheet sizes such as Crown, Demy, Royal, or international paper sizes (appendix 3). For convenience and speed of printing, sheets may be larger than the broadsheet size, thus Double Crown or Quad Crown, etc, when they are termed multiples

The basic unit of a book is called a section. Sections are formed when the printed sheet is subdivided by folding, or by cutting and folding, with due regard to the printed imposition and pagination (page numbering). Besides the subdivision of sheets into the common Crown Octavo or Demy Octavo section sizes, subdivisions can offer a widely

 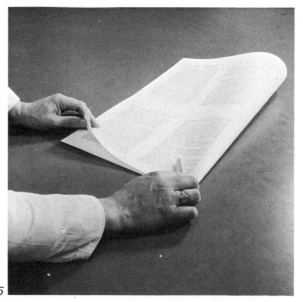

14　15

varied section range using either long or short measure binding-edges to provide both upright (common) or oblong (landscape) format.

15–18 show the folding of a Demy broadsheet to Demy Octavo. The sheet is printed with eight pages on each side and will make a 16-page section. The sheet is positioned with its lowest page number facing downwards at the bottom left-hand corner. Using a bone-folder, three successive folds are then made, each at right angles to the previous and each fold halving a long edge. The second fold or bolt is slit with the bone-folder, in from its open end to just beyond centre (*17*), thus preventing creasing inside the section when the third and final fold is made. Note how the corner of the sheet is raised slightly so that facing pages can be sighted accurately into position (folding to print)

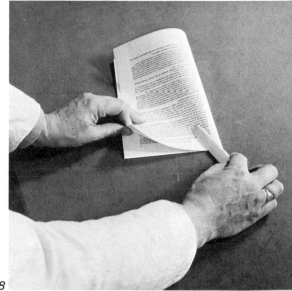

18

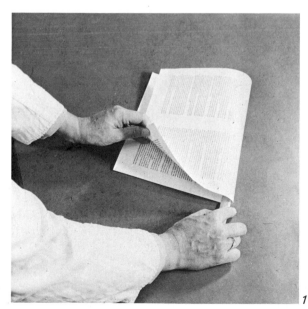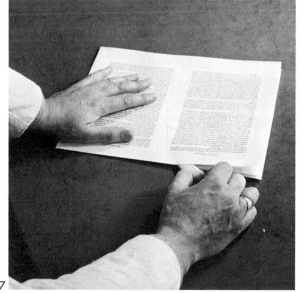

16 17

19

19 Most sheets are identified by an alphabetical or numerical signature-mark printed in sequence at the foot of the lowest numbered page, i.e. the first page of each folded section. Alphabetical sequences normally adhere to tradition and use the old twenty-three letter alphabet, omitting J V and W. The half-title page is normally considered sufficient identification in itself for the first section. 2A or Aa indicates that there are more than twenty-three sections and that the alphabet is being used for a second sequence. B* would indicate that two sections are to be inserted one within the other, the outer section carrying the normal signature B. Signatures identify the sheet, help in positioning for folding, identify the folded section and help during the gathering of the sections into order. They can also help when checking section order for accuracy while collating (*26*).

Specifically a collating aid is the back-mark, printed to position on the back-folds of sections and form series of steps, a break in which will instantly indicate a misplaced section.

20 After folding, gathered sections are knocked-up to their heads and back-folds and placed between pressing-boards and into a nipping or standing-press to consolidate. Any tendency for the sections to slip can be avoided by reducing their numbers, perhaps by dividing a complete gathering into halves

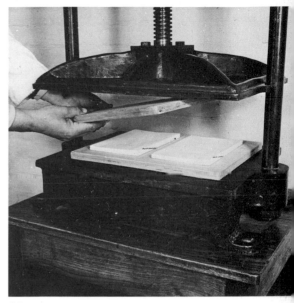

20

21   A single-section case-binding
     A multi-section case-binding
     A quarter-leather library-style binding

Multi-section case-binding

Proceeding with pressed sections as in figure *20* the following sequences demonstrate a multi-section case-binding. In case-binding the body of the book is built-up quite separately from its cover or case. The two parts are joined together in a final operation called casing-in.

Preparing for sewing

22   The pressed sections, with strawboard on either side, have been knocked-up carefully to their head and back-edges and placed (head to the left) in a bench-press ready for marking-up. The book is Demy Octavo format made-up of 18 sixteen-page sections

23   Three $\frac{1}{2}$ inch width tapes are positioned so that they divide the head to tail measurement into four equal parts

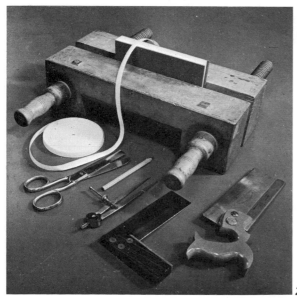
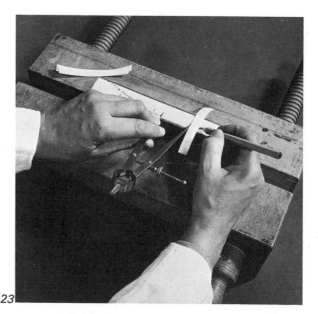

22   23

24   The tape positions are clearly marked across the back-folds together with marks one tape-width in from head and tail for the kettlestitches (chain stitches linking section to section)

25   The kettlestitch marks are sawn-in to a depth of about $\frac{1}{16}$ inch to accommodate the kettlestitches

26   The sections are collated by checking the signatures for correct order immediately prior to sewing

26

24   25

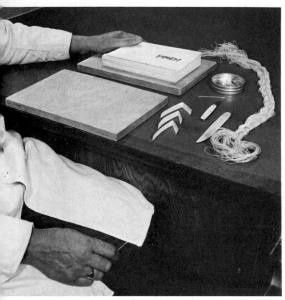

27

Sewing

27   The sewer is seated sideways to the bench. The three tapes shown ready are about $2\frac{1}{2}$ inches longer than the book is thick. The thread is 16-2 cord gauge. The bookbinder's needle is a Number 18

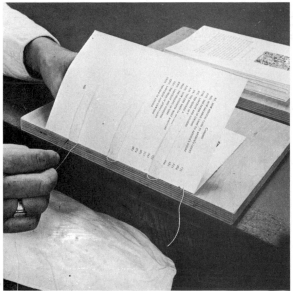

28

28 The first section is faced down on the pressing-board and the tapes are placed to their marks with about one-third of their length tucked under the section. Sewing begins at the head kettlestitch position with the thread passing in and out of the back-fold and over the tapes in succession

29 The needle is passed out from the first section and into the second section through the tail kettlestitch positions. The left hand works inside the section in taking the needle, turning it round and pushing it out, whilst the right hand works similarly outside of the section

30 When the second section has been sewn the long and short ends of thread are drawn taut and tied together with a reef-knot, i.e. right over left and under, left over right and under

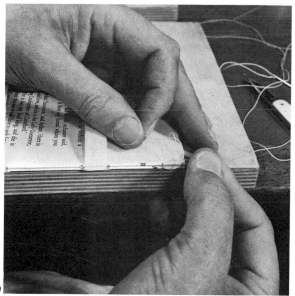

29 30

31 The thread is being drawn taut when the sewing of the third section is complete. To prevent tearing, draw threads taut in-line with the back-folds of sections and not at right angles

32–33 From the completion of the third section, kettle-stitches can be worked at head and tail. To make a kettle-stitch and thus tie down a section the needle is taken under the previous section sewn, out at the tail or head (whichever is the case) and up through the loop thus formed

34 The sewing is tapped-down with a bone-folder every few sections to keep it as firm as possible

31   32

33

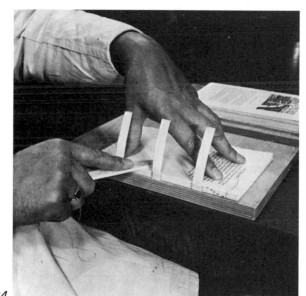

34

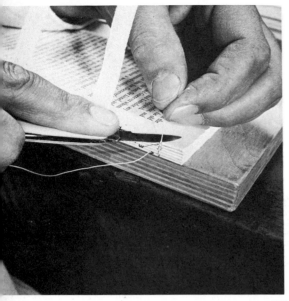

35 The head kettlestitch has been worked around the short end of thread left at the commencement of the sewing of the first section (*28* and *30*) and this end is now cut off after six sections have been sewn

36 The needle can be conveniently rested while both hands are occupied finding the centre of the next section

37–38 A new thread is tied-on using a sheet-bend. A loop is made in the old thread. The new thread does all the moving. It crosses the loop (*37*), goes round behind the loop, under itself and then through the loop (*38*). The two ends of the old and the two ends of the new thread are drawn tight and the short ends of each are cut as close to the knot as possible. Knots should be arranged so that they can be pulled through the saw-cut of a kettlestitch position and so rest in the fold of the section

35

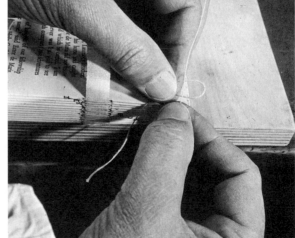

36　37

39 A double kettlestitch is made when the sewing is finished. The thread is then spiralled down the kettlestitches to a depth of six sections and cut off flush

40 The needle holes are rubbed down with a bone-folder to prevent glue penetrating into the sections at a later stage

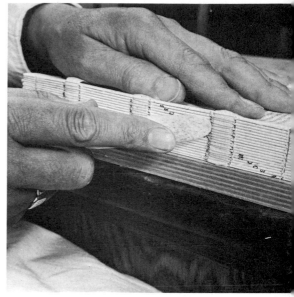

40

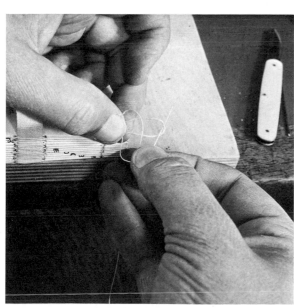

38 39

Swell

Sewing creates swell in what is now the back of the book. Swell helps to give the book shape at the rounding and backing stages (*48–56*). Swell is largely dependent upon the choice of sewing thread thickness in relation to the number and make-up of the sections. The amount of swell that should be aimed for to give the book a desired shape varies, depending upon the width or bulk of the body of the book and the height of the backing-joint required.

41 Using a knocking-down iron and hammer to reduce the swell in the back of the book until it is about one-quarter greater than the mean width at the foredge

Endpapering

42   A pair of cartridge endpapers with head to tail machine-direction are cut and folded. The cartridge paper being used is of Double Demy 60 lb substance

43 $\frac{1}{8}$ inch of the endpapers are exposed from under waste newspaper and their folds are pasted. The endpapers are then pitched precisely level with the head and back-folds of the first and last sections of the book and rubbed down with the fingers. This type of attachment is called tipping-on

44   The endpapered book is placed between boards and under a weight for a quarter of an hour

42   43

Back gluing

45 With pieces of strawboard on either side, the book is knocked-up carefully to its back and head and placed into a bench-press. The back is glued-up with thin, hot, flexible glue which is brushed thoroughly between the sections. After gluing, the book is removed from the press and put to one side, with its glued area just off a pressing-board. It should be dry and ready for cutting in half an hour

45

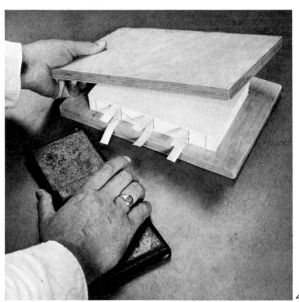

44

46

47

Cutting

As little as possible should be removed from the leaves when cutting edges, particularly in the case of books being re-bound. With new and uncut sections consideration should be given to the page layout and the planned proportion of its margins. An allowance is likely to be made for the removal of $\frac{1}{8}$ inch from the shortest leaves of uncut sections. Before cutting any book, a check should be made for text or illustrations printed close to the edges and also the possible presence of any folded plates or maps. When using either a single-knife guillotine or a press and plough, edges are normally cut in the order of foredge, tail and head. A book is said to be 'trimmed' if the knife touches the longer leaves only and 'cut' if it touches every leaf.

46 A power-operated single-knife guillotine for cutting paper and book edges. Guillotines vary in detail but each essentially consists of a bed on which the work rests, a back-gauge which determines the depth of cut, a clamp which holds the work firm and a knife suspended from a carriage. The knife descends and makes a cut, thence returning to its rest position. Qualified instruction should be obtained personally in the correct and safe use of any guillotine that may be available to a reader

47 The head of this book has been cut in a guillotine. The book edge rests on a nylon cutting-stick set into the bed of the machine. Under the clamp and resting on top of the book is a fanned-out pad of paper preventing the swell in the back of the book from becoming crushed. The knife has returned to its rest position leaving the off-cut of paper from the edge of the book in the foreground of the photograph

An alternative method of cutting book edges using cutting-press and plough is shown in figures *147–150*.

Rounding

48–49 Rounding the book to its traditional shape using hammer and fingers. In this operation the effect of the correct amount of swell left in the back after sewing will be noted. The round should be of an even arc. If the glue has become too set it should be softened by dampening with a sponge about five minutes before commencing to round the book

49

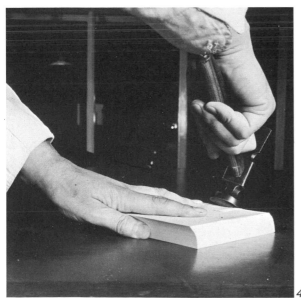
48

50

Edge colouring

50　The top-edge or head of the book may be coloured with powder or poster colour mixed with thin paste and applied with a pad of cotton-wool worked along the edge from back to foredge. After a few minutes drying, the book can be removed from between the waste strawboards and from under the weight

51

Backing

51 The backing-height measure for case-binding is twice the thickness of the strawboard to be used for the cover. This measure is marked from the fold of the endpapers at head and tail

52 The backing-boards are adjusted to the backing-height mark

53 The book, with backing-boards set, is lowered into a lying-press which is screwed up as tightly as possible with its press-pin. Should the backing-boards slip whilst putting the book into the press it will be necessary to take it out again and re-set the backing-boards. Persistent slipping may be cured by dampening the inner face of the backing-boards. Lying-presses rest horizontally about 30 inches above floor-level on a support called a press-tub

52   53

54 In backing, the sections are knocked gently outwards with light glancing blows from the face, and later the toe (*55*) of the backing-hammer. Roughly one-third of the sections are hammered to the left and one-third to the right, the centre third of the sections remaining virtually untouched by the hammer. On removal from the press the backing joints may be neatly sharpened against strawboards with a bone-folder (*56*)

Rounding and backing together deal with the problem of swell occasioned by sewing. Rounding distributes the swell over an arc. It produces a convex back which is aesthetically pleasing, together with a concave foredge eminently suited to opening. Backing fully distributes the swell. It helps to set and consolidate the round of the book. It provides definite joints from which the cover boards will hinge and its bending outwards of the back-folds of the sections is an aid to flat opening of the leaves.

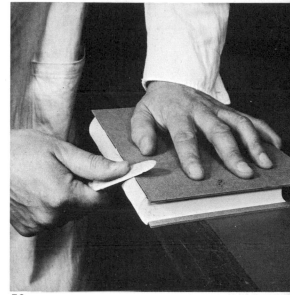

56

55

Back-lining

57–62 demonstrate back-lining. A first lining of mull and a second lining of kraft paper are used to give strength to the joints and back of the book

57 The mull is cut to size 1 inch in width beyond each joint and $\frac{1}{8}$ inch short of the edges at head and tail. The back is thinly but thoroughly brushed with Scotch glue or a cold P.V.A. adhesive worked carefully off the edges. The mull is positioned and rubbed down with a folder

58 Kraft paper is measured to the exact width of the back

57

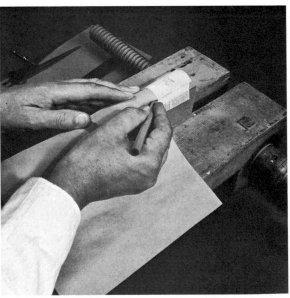

58 59

59 Two strips of the kraft paper with head to tail machine-direction are cut a little longer than the back of the book. One piece should be kept aside to act as a hollow-strip or case lining during case-making and it will be cut to the head to tail measure of the boards, when this is known. The strips are shown being cut on a piece of millboard using a penknife and a steel straight-edge

60 The back is given a second gluing

61 The kraft paper second lining is positioned and rubbed down

62 The kraft paper is cut flush with head and tail

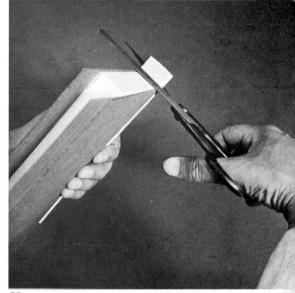
62

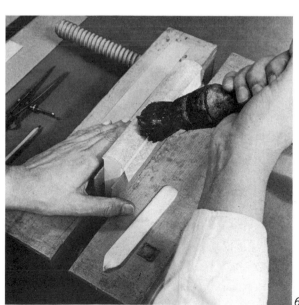

60 61

43

63 The slips of tape are trimmed level with the edge of the mull, thus completing the work on the body of the book

Squaring boards

64 It will have been noted that from the completion of backing, the book has been kept continually between an oversize pair of strawboards to protect its joints. After cutting one long and one short edge to a right angle, the strawboards are marked for size. With the good back-edge of board placed comfortably into the joint, the square (projection) of the board at head, tail and foredge, is judged equal to the board's own thickness. The strawboard being used is $1\frac{1}{2}$ lb or $0\cdot072$ in. thickness (appendix 4)

65–66 A board cutter. The example shown is a heavy-duty cutter but this type of machine is available in smaller sizes. It consists of a bed, side-lay with rule, back-gauge, foot-operated clamp and two blades, one fixed and the other pivoted

Boards can also be cut with a press and plough or with a small cutting-press and knife as shown in figure *67*.

63 64

67

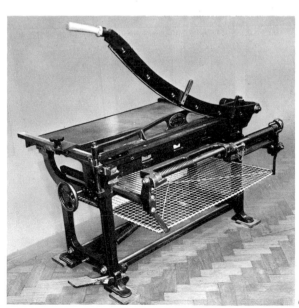

65 66

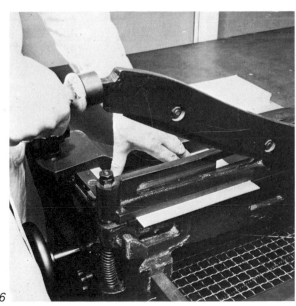

45

Cutting cover materials

68   Cutting the bookcloth covering material. Woven fabrics should normally be cut so that the joint of the book is parallel with the selvedge of the roll. There is greater resistance to opening if the warp threads (i.e. those running up the length of the roll) are allowed to cross the joints. The selvedge itself, being uneven, is cut off. Fibre-felt or paper covering materials should be cut with their machine-directions running from head to tail. The covering material is cut wider than the board edges to allow for a $\frac{5}{8}$ inch turn-in all round

Case-making

69   The bench laid out for case-making. At the back: pressing-boards, weight, the book with boards set into the joints but knocked flush with the edge at the tail, a piece of kraft paper for rubbing-down, a pot of hot case-making glue with $1\frac{1}{2}$ inch glue-brush. To the left: the kraft paper hollow-strip, pencil, shears, bone-folder. To the right: the bookcloth covering material (with the position of one board marked) lying face-side downwards on a piece of waste newspaper

68

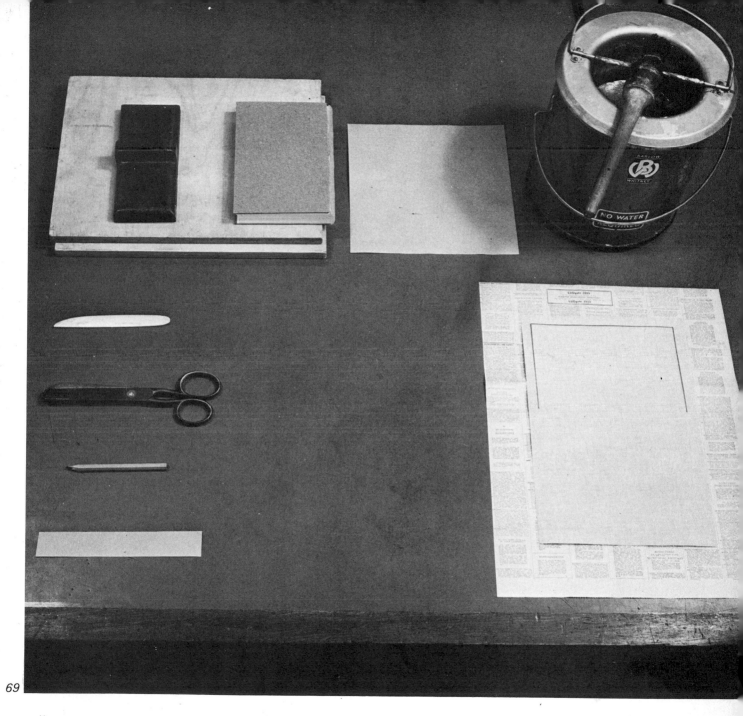

70–71 The case-making glue should be thin enough to run freely from the brush. The brush should be well charged and worked over the cloth as indicated by the arrows, using an even dabbing-out action rather than with dragged brush strokes. Alternative adhesives for this operation are a Scotch glue and paste mixture, or a P.V.A. glue. The glued cloth is then transferred to the clear bench space shown in figure *69*. The cloth is best lifted with middle fingers on the glued side and thumbs on the face side. The fingers should be wiped clean immediately

72 The book is positioned on the glued bookcloth

73 The hollow-strip is positioned

74 The book and boards are held firm and the cloth is drawn tightly around the back and then rubbed down with the palms on to the upper board

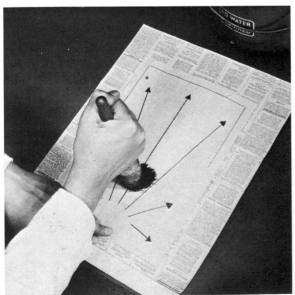 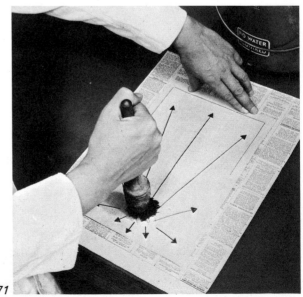

70 71

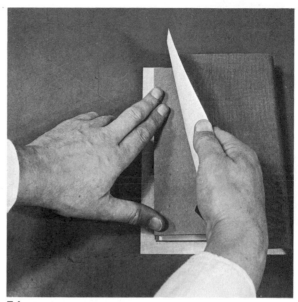

74

72   73

49

75 The upper board (now attached to the cloth) is thrown back and marked to face the endpaper paste-down leaf

76 The corners of the cloth are cut at 45 degrees, about $1\frac{1}{2}$ times board thickness away from the strawboard corner

77 Folding the turn-in tightly to the board edge

78 Pulling the turn-in over with fingers and rubbing-down with bone-folder

79 Nicking-down with finger-nail the small piece of cloth left at the board corners, before turning-in the foredge

80 Rubbing-down the face-side of the made case with bone-folder, through a piece of kraft paper

81 Checking the fit of the case around the body of the book. The spine of the case may be rubbed down flat through kraft paper after the check has been made and then the case placed between pressing-boards and under a weight to dry out

75

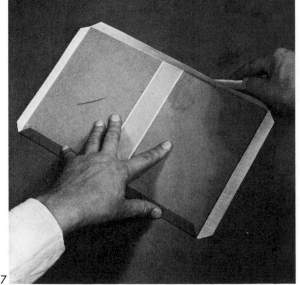

76 77

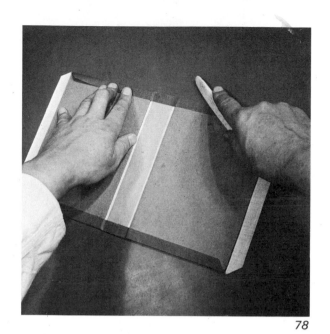

78

79

80

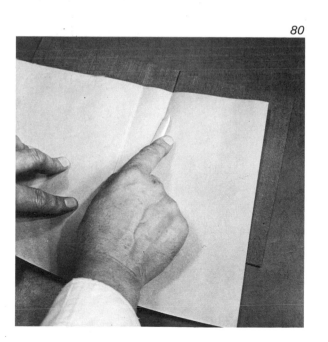

81

Tooling with foil

The use of foil for lettering is a comparatively simple process requiring no preliminary treatment of the covering material. Foil is composed of gold, aluminium or pigment, sandwiched between a carrier film (such as Melinex) on its upper side and a heat-sensitive adhesive on the side placed to the work. Lettering or decoration is effected by impressing a heated metal die (either in the form of a hand-tool or a block) on to the upper side of the foil. This activates the adhesive and a gold or coloured impression of the die used is left in the covering material.

82 A bench laid out for lettering. Included in the layout is a pad of paper on which titling arrangements may be written, a set of handle-letters placed in alphabetical order around the gas-heated finishing stove, a pad of wet cotton-wool in a saucer for cooling and a further pad of dry cotton-wool for cleaning off. (It should be noted that for convenience in photographing these lettering sequences the stove was moved from its normal permanent position on a fixed piece of asbestos sheet)

83 A handle-letter on the finishing stove, showing the nick cut across its shank to indicate the top of the letter

84 Using the cooling-pad of wet cotton-wool. If the tool does not sizzle it is too cool. When the tool does sizzle it should be kept on the pad until the sizzle just stops, when it is ready for use

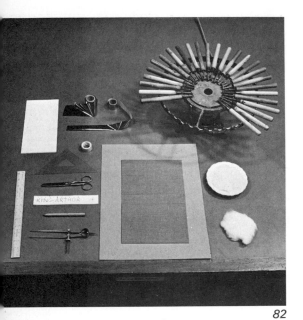

82

83

85 Impressing a handle-letter through Whiley's ZRO gold foil held to the spine of the case by transparent adhesive tape. The foil has been marked-up with a guide-line and ticks made lightly on its surface with a point of the dividers. The top of the letters touch the guide-line. The ticks are spaced equally along the guide-line but letters may require placing slightly to the left or right of their tick depending upon their particular width and shape, so that the spaces left between letters appear to be optically even. Pressure required will vary depending upon the size of the face of the letter, but should be only just enough to obtain a good impression into the particular covering material used. Large sized letters and decorative tools will require a slight rocking of the handle in order to get the impression solid all over. If the tools used are too cool, the gold or colour will be incomplete, or entirely absent. If the tools are too hot the gold or colour may fill-in or even extend beyond the actual face area. If this happens, the impression may be cleared using the dampened point of a sharpened match-stick. Incomplete impressions can be made good by covering the particular area with foil and re-tooling. The finished work may be rubbed off with dry cotton-wool to remove any flecks of gold or pigment from the cover surface

84

Whilst tooling is the manual application of heated metal dies to the cover surface, blocking is their mechanical application. The dies used for mechanically applied impressions are called blocks. Blocking is used when the size of die required is too large for manual application or when the quantity of work being produced is numerous and repetitive.

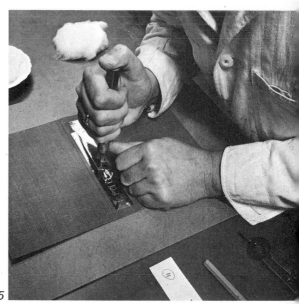

85

Blocking with foil

86 shows two brass blocks attached with glued brown paper to the heat-plate of a hand-operated electrically heated blocking-press

87 shows a blocked case ready for removal from the sliding bed of the press. The heat-plate and blocks are in their operating position under the heat-box. The gold foil is automatically fed downwards from its reels and then between the blocks and the case to the back of the machine

Blocking can also be carried out with the use of brass type locked into a chase which is then screwed to the heat-plate.

86 87

54

Casing-in and pressing

88 Pulling the finished case gently up and down over the edge of the bench to round its spine

89 Waste newspaper under the endpaper paste-down leaf protects the book edges during casing-in. The slips of tape and the mull are pasted but an excessive amount of adhesive in the joint should be avoided as it will squeeze out under pressure

89

88

90–92 The case is closed on to the paste-down leaves, the squares are adjusted if necessary (by sliding the body) and the book is placed between boards and into press. The press used is the nipping-press shown in figure *4*. A larger press for flat pressing is known as a standing-press but the one illustrated is more than adequate for this operation. The book is slightly out from centre to reduce pressure across the joints. Pressure should be reasonably firm at first but may be reduced after about an hour. It is ideal if books can remain in the press overnight

90

91 92

Opening

93   On removal from press the boards are opened and the endpaper fly-leaf is folded back to its paste line

94   Opening of the body of the book should be done by simultaneously taking a few leaves from the front and the rear of the book, working gradually towards its centre and thus easing the back-linings

The case-bound book is now completed and ready for use.

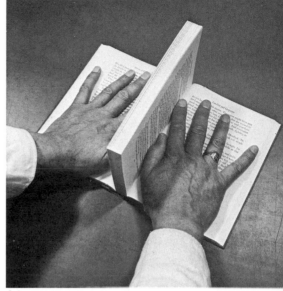

94

93

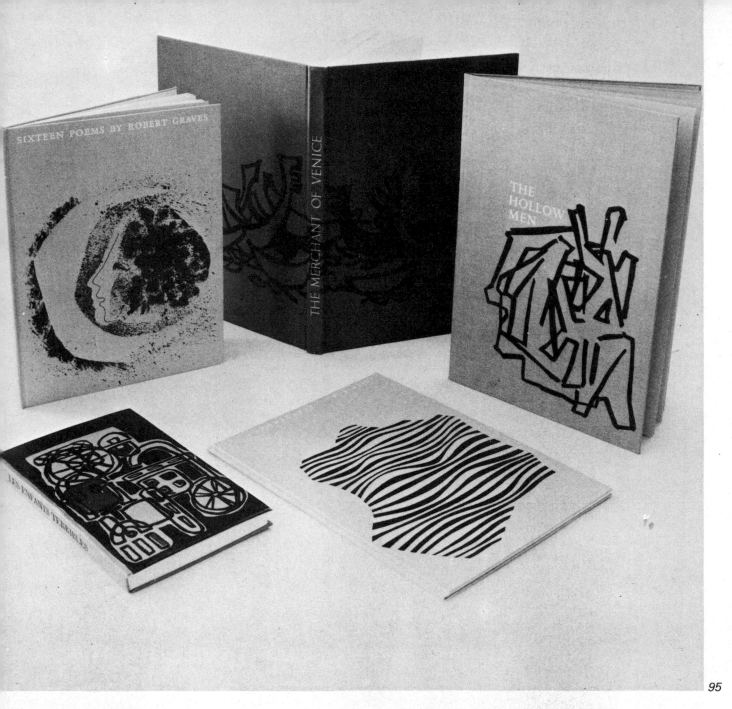

95

Pre-printed cases

95 A group of case-bound books produced by students at the Oxford College of Technology. The bookcloth was pre-printed by offset-lithography before being made-up into a case. The cases were then blocked in gold or pigment foil using brass type. *Les Enfants Terribles* in the left foreground and *The Merchant of Venice* at the rear, although multi-section bindings, had too few sections to warrant rounding and backing. They were therefore left square-back with the boards set $\frac{1}{4}$ inch from the fold of the endpapers

Making decorated papers

96–102 show simple methods for making decorative papers which may then be effectively used as endpapers or as board siding papers

96

Paste papers

96   Paste, coloured with poster paint, is applied to cartridge paper

97–98   Combs cut from millboard are used to make formal or free patterns, as desired

99   Dryad printing sticks being used to impress patterns into the paste. Interesting results can also be obtained by rolling the sticks across the paper. In effect, anything that will activate the brushed paste can be utilised into service. The papers need to be kept between boards when dry

97

98   99

60

Relief printing

100 Torn and cut pieces of mull being placed on a glued millboard to produce a relief printing surface. Other materials such as teased-out string, sacking, glass paper, corrugated paper and leaves may be used

101 The relief surface is rolled with printing ink

102 Cartridge paper placed on the inked surface is rubbed down by hand and then carefully removed. Superimposed prints can be made using the same or other coloured inks and from the same or alternative reliefs

Coloured paper can be used successfully for both types of decorated papers.

102

100 101

Case-binding variants

The case made in figures *68–81* is in full cloth.

103   shows some variations in case-making using cloth and decorative papers

Back left quarter cloth with paper sides

Back centre quarter cloth with paper sides turned-in on the back-edge

Back right paper case with head and tail cloth strip

Front left half cloth with paper sides

Front right half cloth with paper sides and cloth foredge strip

104   Quarter cloth with paper sides. The cloth spine is turned-in at head and tail over the board edges and hollow-strip. A paper side normally overlaps the cloth by $\frac{1}{8}$ inch. Its corners are treated as in figure *76*

105   Quarter cloth with paper sides turned-in on the back-edge. The hollow-strip is glued to the cloth spine, the head and tail turn-ins of which are glued and rubbed down. A pencil line is made on the cloth to mark the board position. The paper side, which may conveniently have its corners pre-cut as indicated, is glued to the board and its back-edge only is turned-in. The cloth is glued up to the pencil line to receive the board which is then pitched to position. The head, tail and finally the foredge of the paper side is then turned-in. A quick nip in the press between pressing-boards protected with white newsprint ensures good adhesion of the boards

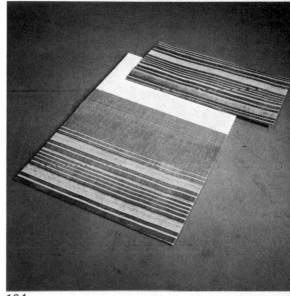

104

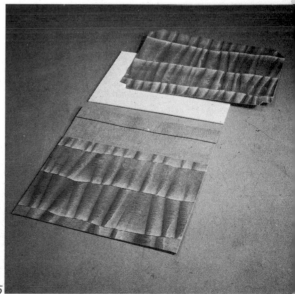

105

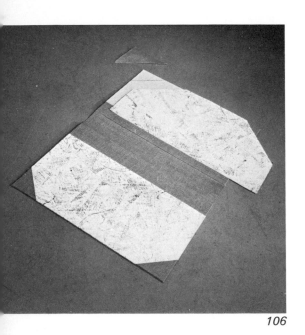

106 Half cloth with paper sides. The pencil line marked for the position of the cloth corner is measured at 45 degrees in from the corner of the board and should traditionally correspond with the amount by which the spine strip overlaps the back-edge, this proportion being usually between one-quarter and one-fifth of the board width

107 Half cloth with paper sides and cloth foredge strips. The proportion of the various components can be varied at will

108 Paper case with head and tail cloth strips. The paper spine strip (without turn-in), overlaps the inside of the boards by about $\frac{3}{4}$ inch and reinforces the paper cover. The head and tail strips show most effectively if they are very narrow. The paper cover is turned-in on its foredge only. Decorative paste-papers are unsuitable for this style as they are likely to crack at the joints

106

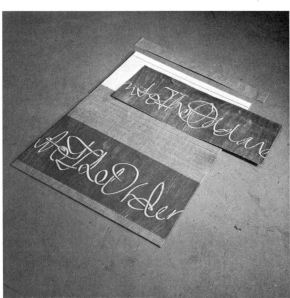

107 108

Single-section case-binding

109 Two 4-page cartridge endpapers are cut, folded and outset around a single-section book. A piece of mull is cut to reinforce the back-fold

110 A paring-stone (lithographic stone, marble or plate-glass surface) is glued out with thin Scotch or P.V.A. adhesive. The mull is placed on the glued surface and rubbed down through waste newspaper. It is then lifted and drawn around the endpapered section using a fold of kraft paper

109 110

111 A bodkin is used to pierce three holes through the back-fold, in the centre and 1 inch from head and tail

112 The thread passes out through the centre hole, in at the head and down the fold, out at the tail and back through the centre, where the ends are tied across the long stitch using a reef-knot

113 Boards for this style are cut with normal squares but their back-edges are set $\frac{1}{4}$ inch from the back-fold of the book. Cases are made without a hollow strip

111

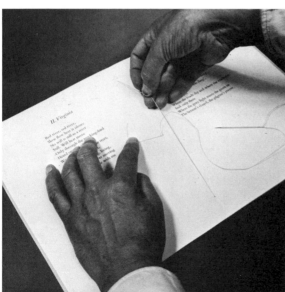

112 113

Preparing a book for re-binding

Dissecting

114 An old case-binding is to be re-bound in a quarter-leather library-style binding. A penknife is stropped before use

115 The endpaper fly-leaf is pulled back and the book is cut from its case by slitting through the mull

116 Loose back-linings are removed

116

114 115

117

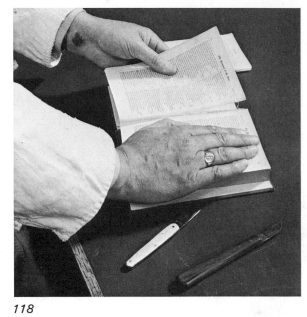

118

119

120

117–118   Threads are cut at the centre of sections which are then pulled firmly away from the body of the book

119–120   Glue fragments are cleaned from the back-folds

121   The old backing grooves are gently hammered-out four sections at a time on the knocking-down iron

121

Guarding

122 Guards for repairing the weakened back-folds of sections are marked out on a sheet of 11 lb white bank paper

123 A knife and straight-edge is used to cut the guards, $\frac{3}{8}$ to $\frac{1}{2}$ inch in width with the machine-direction running along their lengths

124 Paste is off-set on to the guards from the surface of a paring-stone

122

123 124

125–127 The pasted guards are taken from the stone and drawn around the back of sections

Guarding should be adequate to ensure a strong book. Discretion should be exercised in the guarding of books containing numerous thin sections, where over guarding may create a problem of undue swell.

127

125 126

Attaching plates

128–130 A single-leaf plate is pasted $\frac{1}{8}$ inch along the back-edge of its reverse side. A guard is attached to the pasted edge and the plate is allowed to dry-out between boards. The guard is then folded and hooked around a section, from which it will hinge freely after sewing

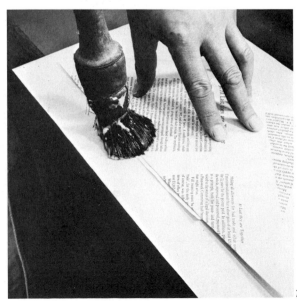

128 129

131 For a library-style binding, $\frac{1}{2}$ inch width tapes cut from cotton label-cloth have been attached with paste to the first and last sections. Two-thirds of the width of each tape has been brought around the section but left unpasted at this stage, being tipped to a cloth-jointed endpaper after sewing (*145*). Guarded and taped sections should be allowed to dry thoroughly before pressing (*20*)

131

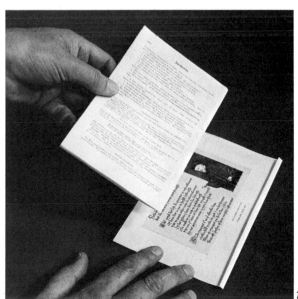

130

73

Quarter-leather library-style binding

The library-style binding to be demonstrated will have its boards attached before covering and so offer a contrast in construction with that of the case-binding.

Cloth-jointed endpapers

132 A cloth-jointed endpaper requires one 1 inch width strip of good quality bookcloth, two 4-page folds of white cartridge paper and two single leaves of coloured Cobb paper. These materials should be doubled to make a pair of endpapers

132

133 134

133 The cloth joints are glued out with a mixture of Scotch glue and paste or a P.V.A. glue (either adhesives are suitable for making this endpaper). One fold of cartridge paper is pitched to cover two-thirds of the width of the cloth and the other pitched to cover the remaining one-third. There should be a $\frac{1}{16}$ inch gap between the folds

134–136 The single leaves of Cobb paper (cut so that they overlap the cloth by $\frac{1}{8}$ inch) are glued-out and lined-in. A piece of white card called a fence prevents the linings from sticking together when the endpapers are given a light quick nip in the press. After being removed from the press the endpapers should be allowed to dry thoroughly between boards and under a weight

137 The endpapers, positioned with the two-thirds width of cloth away from the book, provide a waste leaf, a paste-down leaf, a coloured lined fly-leaf and a white fly-leaf

137

135 136

Marking-up for sewing

138–139   The Crown Octavo book is to be sewn on four $\frac{1}{2}$ inch width tapes. Marks are made $\frac{1}{8}$ inch from head and tail and between these the back is divided into five equal parts. The tape width position is marked to the head side of each one-fifth division. (After covering in leather this will provide a tail panel of greater depth than the remaining panels.) Saw-cuts for the kettlestitches are made $\frac{3}{8}$ inch from head and tail. The endpapers should not be sawn-in

138 139

Sewing on a frame

A sewing-frame can be used to provide greater control when sewing a thick book, or convenience when sewing several books marked-up with identical tape positions. Sewing keys hold firm the lower end of tapes which are passed through the slot in the frame and pinned over the cross-bar.

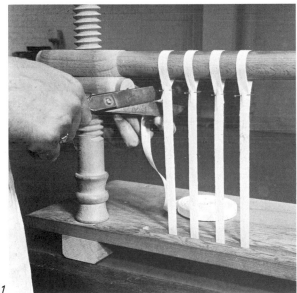

141

140

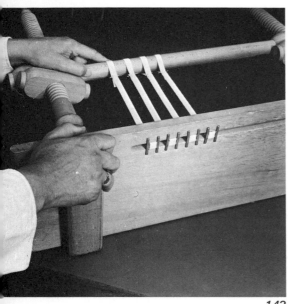

140–144 show the setting up and use of a sewing-frame. The actual sewing process is as described for case-binding, with the exception that the endpapers are sewn through their cloth-joints as though they were sections. If several books are sewn on the frame at one time, each should be sewn independently of the next. When the sewing of a stack of books is completed, their tapes may be slid through the sewing and cut off to give slips of suitable length. Allowance should be made for this when setting up the frame

After sewing, the needle holes are rubbed down and the swell is reduced as in figures *40–41*.

142

143 144

145 The cotton reinforcement strips (*131*) are pasted and the endpapers are carefully positioned on to them. The book is then placed between boards and under a weight for a quarter of an hour (*44*). It is then glued up as in figure *45*

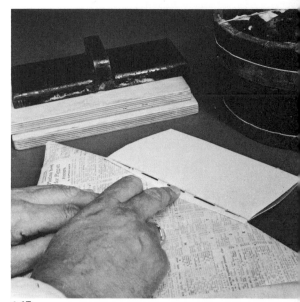

145

Split-boards

146 An 8 oz strawboard is glued to an 8d millboard (see appendix 4) with P.V.A. glue or a mixture of Scotch glue and paste. The strawboard is shown covering about 1½ inches of the width of the millboard while the latter is being glued-out. The strawboard is then turned over head to tail and placed down on the millboard, the unglued portion of which will form the split. Made split-boards should be pressed overnight

Cutting with press and plough

147 The cutting edge of a plough knife

148 At top left a plough is standing on end showing its knife in position. The runners for the plough are seen screwed to the top of a lying-press thus converting it into a cutting-press. The book has been tied with tape to keep it square. The amount to be cut off the foredge has been measured from the

146

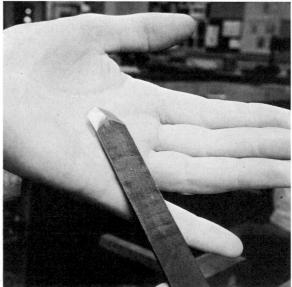

147

back and marked on the endpaper. A cutting-board is being placed to this mark and when in the press will be flush with the top of the right-hand cheek. The cutting-board on which the book rests is protected by a piece of millboard and will remain slightly above the edge to act a 'cut against'

149 As the plough is worked forwards and backwards its screw is slowly turned, advancing the knife which gradually cuts across the book edge

150 To avoid problems of swell, the book should be rounded and backed before getting it into the press to cut head and tail. A backing height of one and a half times the thickness of the split-boards is normal for this style. The head as shown has been cut, and the off-cut clinging to the sections at the turn of the backing is being removed with a sharp knife

150

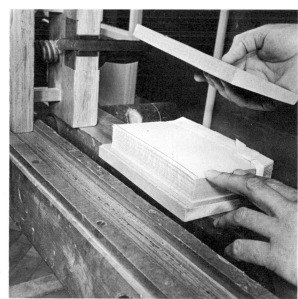

148 149

81

Sprinkling

151–152   Sprinkling is a common form of edge treatment for library bindings. Poster colour mixed with paste and thinned with water is prepared in a basin. An unbridled glue brush is dipped into the colour and twirled between the hands until the bristles are almost dry. The brush is beaten against a press-pin held a few inches from the book and fine spots of colour are transferred to its edges

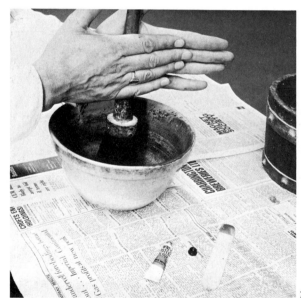

151

152

Setting the back and attaching boards

153 The waste-leaves of the endpapers are glued-out and folded back into the joints, sandwiching the slips of tape. The book is pressed

154 Whilst in the press the back is well pasted and allowed to soak for a few minutes. Then, using a piece of board, paste and surplus glue is scraped from the back which is finally wiped clean with a damp sponge. The book should remain in the press until quite dry. This operation firmly sets the shape of the book

154

153

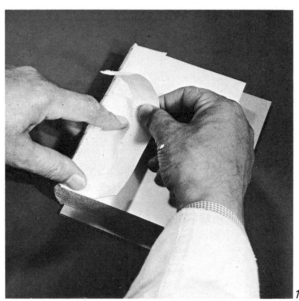

155

156

155 On removal from the press the folded waste-leaves are torn with a feathered edge about 1 inch away from and parallel with the joints. The tongue which remains is shortened at head and tail by 1 inch. This tongue will provide the means of attaching the split-boards to the body of the book

156 When cutting split-boards to size normal squares are given, but there should be a gap allowed between the back-edges and the backing-joints equal to twice the board thickness. This will provide freedom in opening and produce what is known as a 'french joint'

157 The split-board is opened and glued

158 The boards are positioned (thinner board to the book), the squares are set and the book is placed into a nipping or standing press overnight

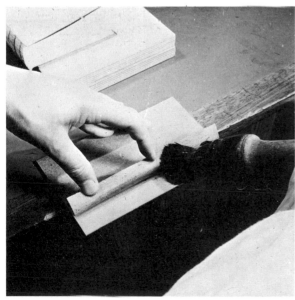

157 158

Knife sharpening

159–162   show the sharpening of a German paring-knife. The knife is bevelled on one edge and flat on the other

159   The bevelled edge is placed to the oil-stone and worked up and down the stone until a burr can be felt on the flat edge of the blade

160   The knife is now reversed and the burr is removed by carefully drawing the flat edge of the blade down the stone

161   Bevelled and flat edges are alternately stropped on a mounted piece of hide to remove any fragments of metal and to produce a keen cutting edge

162   To prevent it damaging the leather when paring, the point of the knife is rounded-off on the side of the oil-stone

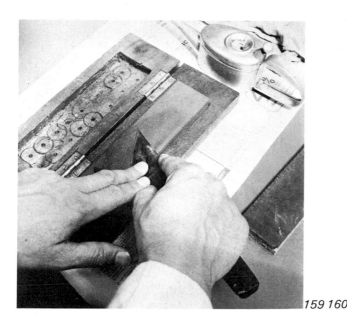 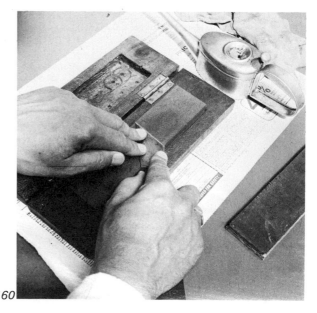

159 160

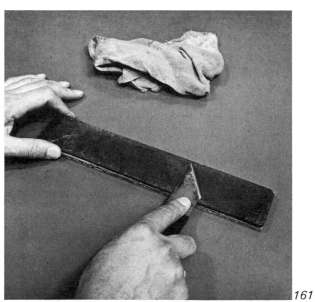

161

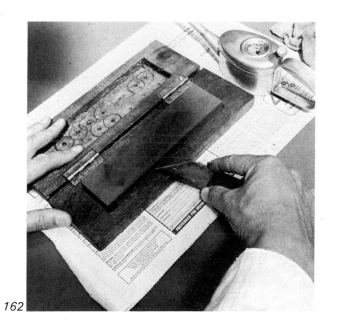

162

163

Leather

A good quality leather remains one of the best materials for covering. Leather can be strong yet supple, pleasant to work, and satisfying to look at and handle. Calf, sheepskin and pigskin are all used for bookbinding purposes but the most popular covering leather among craft-bookbinders is a sumac-tanned, aniline-dyed, Niger morocco type goatskin, resistant to atmospheric pollution.

163 A paper template, large enough to overlap the boards by 1 inch and provide a $\frac{3}{4}$ inch turn-in at head and tail, is used as a guide when cutting leather for the library binding

164

Paring leather

The purpose of paring is to systematically reduce the thickness of leather so that it will function properly, be more easily worked and at the same time provide an acceptable measure of neatness to the finished book. As any reduction in the thickness of leather is a reduction in its strength, paring must be a planned operation.

Old lithographic stones, or marbled slabs, make very suitable paring-stones.

164 shows the line of the joints and the turn-in marked on the under-side of the leather with a soft pencil. Edge-paring begins with a back stroke

165 Making a forward stroke. Movements should be as even as possible. The knife must be sharp and must not saw at the leather. The more the handle is tilted up the greater is the danger of cutting through the leather

166 The knife being used almost flat to remove the ridge from preliminary edging strokes

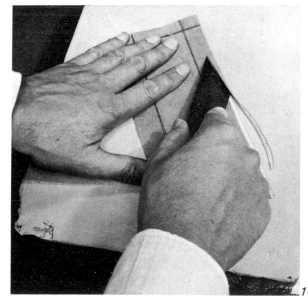 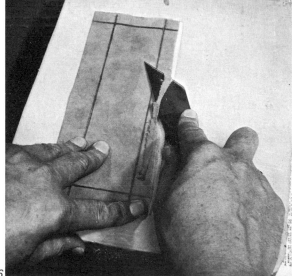

165 166

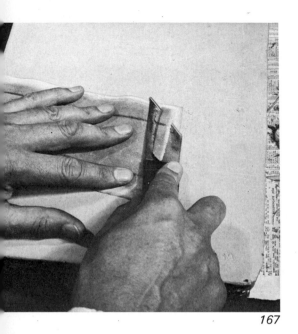

167   The knife being used almost flat to extend the paring at head and tail to just beyond the turn-in mark

168   Using the heel of the knife to fluff-out the leather between the lines of the joints and to the depth of the turn-in so that the latter will not protrude. The turn-in line will require re-marking on the leather together with a further line to control the extent of this paring

169   Fingers feel and check the progress of the paring

170   The heel of the knife may be used to pare along the line of the joints if it is considered that the thickness of the leather will preclude the free opening of the book

171   A spokeshave being used (after edge-paring) to thin down an over-thick piece of leather which is protected with a backing-board while being held to the stone with a G-clamp

172   Using a 'French' paring knife for the same operation as shown in figure 168

167

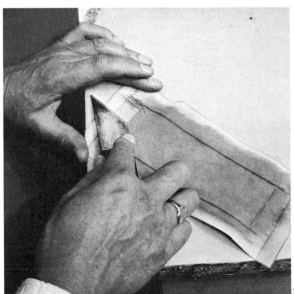

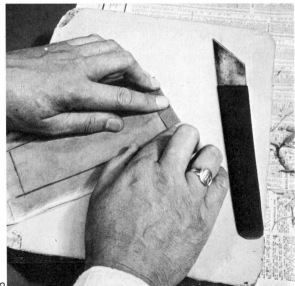

168 169

172

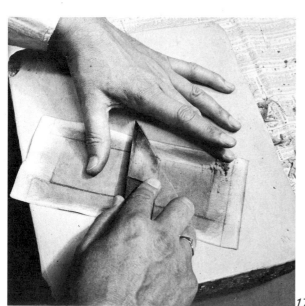

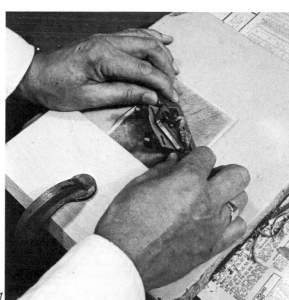

170 171

Covering

173 The leather is dampened with water on its face-side, turned over and pasted-out and, after a few minutes soaking, is re-pasted. The paring-stone will act as a working surface and should be sponged clean as necessary. On the corner of the stone rest two paste-soaked pieces of hemp cord cut to the width of the back and ready for insertion into the turn-in where later they will help form a head-cap. The back of the book is pasted

174 The leather is drawn round the back and pressed down with a bone-folder into the space left between board and backing, thus forming the french joint

173

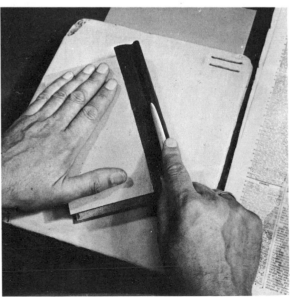

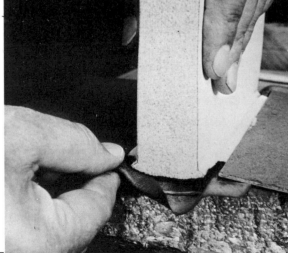

174 175

175 A piece of the pasted hemp is introduced at each turn-in so that it will eventually sit neatly on the edge of the book. The turn-in (which is pasted where it will touch the back of the book), is then brought over the edge of the boards and tucked down the back, leather to leather

176 The turn-in is smoothed to the boards and any surplus of leather worked to the back-edges

177 The spine is rubbed down through kraft paper

178 The book is tied around its joints with hemp cord

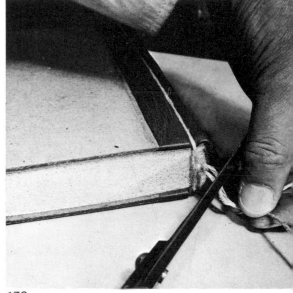

178

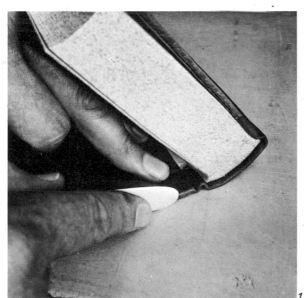

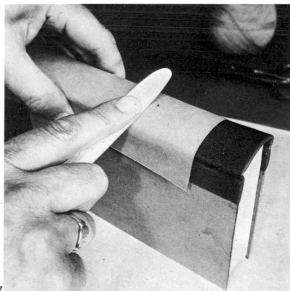

176 177

179 The head-cap is smoothed and shaped at 45 degrees to the head and tail edges

The leather is finally sponged over and the book placed for safety between cartridge paper and pressing-boards until next day, when the cord can be removed, the leather dampened at the joint and the boards opened.

180–182 Trimming-out the edge of the leather will ensure a neat fit of the cloth side

180 A folder mark is made about $\frac{1}{8}$ inch in from the edge of the leather, parallel with and an equal amount in from the back-edge of both boards

181 A small strip is removed from the edge of the leather with a bevelled cut made along the folder mark

182 Cloth sides are cut, glued and pitched up the bevel and into the folder mark

183–184 The cloth sides are turned-in with a 'library-corner'

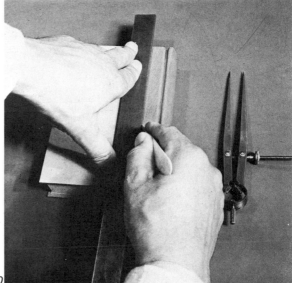

179 180

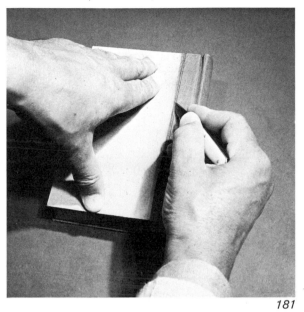

181

182

183

184

Finishing

Blind tooling

This is the application of finishing-tools to a book cover in impression only, without the use of gold or colour.

185   The spine of the quarter-leather library-style binding is divided out into shallow bands and panels. The bands relate to the positions of the tapes on which the book was sewn, and their widths, together with those of the panels, should be checked for accuracy. A tick on the surface of the leather, made with the point of the dividers, will be a suitable mark for aligning the piece of thread, which is drawn left and right across the spine

186   The friction mark left by the thread acts as a guide when a single-line pallet is worked in blind over the spine. A pallet should be heated and cooled in the way shown for a handle-letter in figures *82–84*. If desired, dark impressions can be produced if the leather is dampened slightly and re-worked with a cool tool. Alternatively a pallet line can be polished-in by cooling down the tool and working it backwards and forwards across its original impression

187   A single-line fillet is worked up the leather where it touches the cloth. If over-heated on the finishing-stove a fillet will require cooling under a cold tap. If the wheel is wedged with a small piece of wood it may also be used to polish-in an impressed line. Rolls are similar to fillets in general appearance but their edges are cut with a decorative face

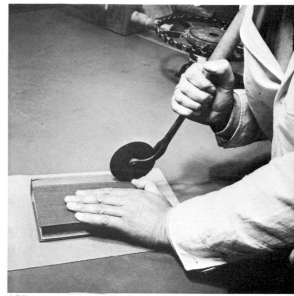

187

185 186

Direct lettering with gold leaf and type

Glaire is an albuminous mordant used when tooling with gold leaf. It is applied wet to a book cover and allowed to dry. Gold leaf is given a temporary attachment to the glaired surface by applying to the latter a little white Vaseline. The glaire congeals under the application of the finishing-tools and thus the gold impression is made. The making of glaire is described in appendix 5.

The Niger morocco library-style binding will require its panel prepared for lettering. It should be sponged with a 50 per cent dilution of vinegar in water and when this is dry, one coat of glaire. When the glaire is dry the panel is lightly greased with white Vaseline applied with a small pad of cotton-wool.

188 189

188–189 A leaf of gold is removed from its book and placed on the calf-suede covered gold cushion. It is gently breathed on to make it flat before being cut into convenient sizes with the thin-bladed gold knife. (A light dressing of bath-brick dust or powdered pumice spread on the cushion with the gold knife will keep both cushion and knife clean and will facilitate the cutting of the gold leaf)

190 A pad of cotton-wool drawn across the hair is used to lift the gold leaf from its cushion and press it down on to the panel. A second thickness of gold may be used with advantage provided the first thickness is breathed on before the second is padded down

191 A piece of thread lightly drawn across the gold will provide a guide-line. An impression of the type on a strip of paper indicates the length to be accommodated so that its beginning can be ticked in the gold

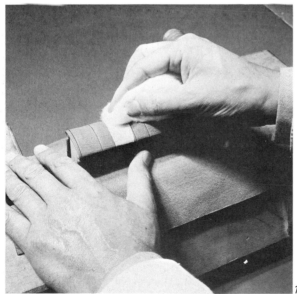 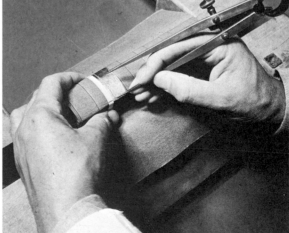

190 191

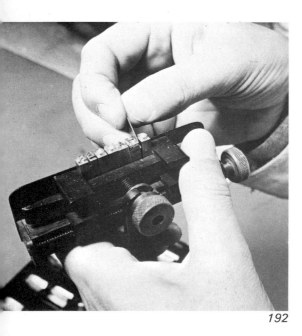

192 The line of brass type is being 'letter-spaced' in a type-holder

193 The type-holder is heated on the finishing stove in the normal way and impressed across the gold

194 After the type is impressed the surplus gold is removed with a specially prepared gold rubber. The panel is finally cleaned of grease and any flecks of gold leaf by the application of a little benzine on cotton-wool

Direct lettering with gold leaf can be carried out on a cloth case-binding. The book to be lettered is first cased-in. The vinegar-water wash is omitted. One coat of glaire is applied.

Lettering in gold leaf with handle-letters and a paper pattern

The lettering is impressed into bank paper cut to the size of the panel. A pencilled guide-line and divider ticks aid in positioning the letters.

192

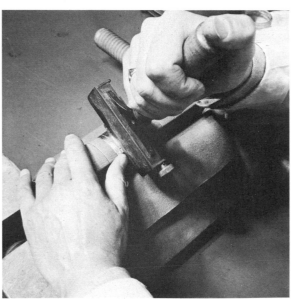

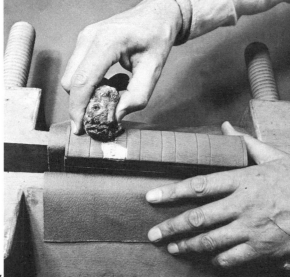

193 194

195 The paper pattern is fixed to the spine of the book with transparent adhesive tape and blind tooling is carried out through the impressions in the pattern. The pattern is removed from the spine which is then re-tooled in blind, directly on the leather, to sharpen the impressions obtained through paper

196 The panel is sponged with vinegar-water and then two coats of glaire are applied to the blind impressions with a fine water-colour brush (an operation commonly known as 'pencilling-in')

When the glaire is dry the panel is greased and at least two layers of gold leaf are padded into the impressions, to ensure that they are completely covered.

197 The final tooling is carried out by working into the impressions seen through the gold leaf, followed by cleaning-off with the gold rubber and benzine. This method of tooling through a paper pattern is adopted when complex decorative patterns are tooled on covers

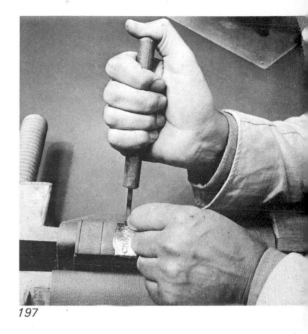

197

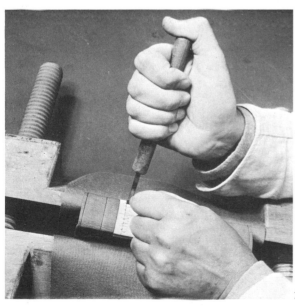

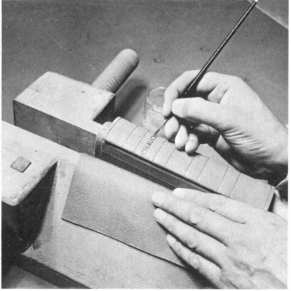

195 196

101

Lettering in panels usually demands some care in the arrangement of space between, above and below lines of lettering. Traditional methods of spacing lines are as follows. For one line of lettering the height of the face to be used is subtracted from the height of the panel and the space remaining is divided into $1\frac{1}{3}$ parts to be used above the line and $1\frac{2}{3}$ parts to be used below the line of lettering.

For more than one line of lettering the height of the face to be used for each line is added together and in total is subtracted from the height of the panel. The space remaining is divided into 1 part between each line of lettering, $1\frac{1}{3}$ parts above the top line and $1\frac{2}{3}$ parts below the bottom line. For example, where two lines of lettering are required, the height of two faces is subtracted from the height of the panel and the remaining space divided in 4 parts (i.e. $1\frac{1}{3}+1+1\frac{2}{3}$), one of the parts being divided into thirds for convenience in re-allocating the space for the lettering layout.

198 Metal edged pressing-boards are shown positioned in the french joints for the final pressing after the endpapers have been pasted-down. The inclusion of a thin card fence placed between the endpaper linings is usual when cloth-jointed endpapers are to be pressed

After pressing, the opening procedure shown in figures *93–94* is carried out. The leather is then polished with a soft duster and the quarter-leather library-style binding is completed.

Appendix 1 *Thread*

Thread is sold by the pound weight. Suitable thicknesses of thread for general use are likely to be 25-2 cord (thin), 16-2 cord (medium) and 16-3 cord (thick).

When a skein of thread is unknotted it will be found to be in circular form; if the circle of thread is cut with shears at the point at which its two ends are knotted it will produce single threads 5 feet in length. These can be made into a plait (7). Threads required for use should be pulled from the loop end of the plait.

Appendix 2 *Paste*

Although prepared paste can be obtained from suppliers, small quantities may be made as follows.

Into a saucepan place 2 ounces of plain flour. Add slowly $\frac{1}{2}$ pint of cold water while stirring with a wooden spoon. Bring to the boil, stirring continually as the mixture thickens. Remove from the stove. Add a pinch of crushed thymol crystals and beat well. The paste can be thinned with boiled water if necessary for a particular operation.

Appendix 3 *Some standard British paper sizes*

Broadsheet	Size in inches
Foolscap	$13\frac{1}{2} \times 17$
Crown	15×20
Large post	$16\frac{1}{2} \times 21$
Demy	$17\frac{1}{2} \times 22\frac{1}{2}$
Medium	18×23
Royal	20×25
Imperial	22×30

Examples of common subdivisions and multiples based on standard broadsheet sizes

Quad Crown	Double Crown	Crown	Crown Folio	Crown Quarto	Crown Octavo
30×40	20×30	15×20	10×15	$7\frac{1}{2} \times 10$	$5 \times 7\frac{1}{2}$
Quad Demy	Double Demy	Demy	Demy Folio	Demy Quarto	Demy Octavo
35×45	$22\frac{1}{2} \times 35$	$17\frac{1}{2} \times 22\frac{1}{2}$	$11\frac{1}{4} \times 17\frac{1}{2}$	$8\frac{3}{4} \times 11\frac{1}{4}$	$5\frac{5}{8} \times 8\frac{3}{4}$

International paper sizes provide a basic sheet for printing papers designated A0 and measuring 841×1189 millimetres in its cut size (approximately $33\frac{1}{8} \times 46\frac{3}{4}$ inches). Subdivisions based on A0 are known as A1, A2, A3, A4, A5 etc. The range A0 to A5 makes an interesting comparison with that of Quad Demy to Demy Octavo.

Appendix 4 *Strawboard and millboard thicknesses*

Traditional designation	Approximate caliper in inches
Strawboard	
8 oz	0·027
12 oz	0·039
16 oz (1 lb)	0·052
24 oz (1½ lb)	0·072
32 oz (2 lb)	0·094
40 oz (2½ lb)	0·121
Millboard	
6d	0·036
7d	0·048
8d	0·064
8d x	0·085
8d xx	0·116
10d (X)	0·144

Appendix 5 *Finishing glaire*

To make

1   Beat one dessertspoonful of vinegar into the white of one large new-laid egg. Allow to stand overnight and then strain through a piece of fine muslin before use.

2   To one dessertspoonful of dried albumen add four dessertspoonfuls of water and one of vinegar. Allow to stand overnight. Stir. Allow to settle and then strain through muslin.

Appendix 6 *Some British and American terms compared*

It would be difficult enough to establish a national standard of technical terms about which all bookbinders could agree, and necessarily even more difficult to compose tables of precisely equivalent terminology as used by craftsmen in two different countries, even though a common language exists between them.

The following is offered as an aid towards understanding. The lists are not comprehensive and are unlikely to be definitive.

British	*American*
Blocking	Stamping
Block	Die
Board cutter	Board shears
Card	Bristol board
Card knife	Mat knife
Carpenter's square	Right-angle gauge
Cartridge paper	Medium-grade book paper
Cotton-wool	Absorbent cotton
Cutting (of book edges)	Trimming
Fence	Barrier sheet
G-clamp	C-clamp
Knocked-up	Jogged
Label cloth	Sized cambric
Millboard	Binder's board
Mull	Super or crash
Plait	Braid
Paste-down (leaf of an end-paper)	Board paper
Reef knot	Square knot
Roll (of tape)	Spool
Scotch glue	Ground glue
Section	Signature
Shoemaker's knife	Utility knife
Signature	Signature mark
Spine (of case or cover)	Backbone or shelfback
Tenon-saw	Backsaw

Suppliers of equipment and materials

Great Britain

Fibre-felt covering materials
Arbofield Products Ltd, 24 Trederwen Road, Hackney, London E.8

Leather
H. Band & Co. Ltd, Brent Way, High Street, Brentford, Middlesex
G. W. Russell and Sons Ltd, The Grange, Bermondsey, London S.E.1

Equipment and sundries
Cefmor-Brehmer Ltd, Tarif Road, London N.17
Dryad Handicrafts, Northgates, Leicester

Marble-paper, finishing stoves and tool handles
Douglas Cockerell & Son Ltd, Riversdale, Grantchester, Cambridge

Adhesives
Croid, Imperial House, 15 Kingsway, London W.C.2

Bookcloth
Thomas Goodall & Co. Ltd, 18 St Swithins Lane, London E.C.4

Leather, equipment and sundries
J. Hewit & Sons Ltd, 97 St John Street, London E.C.1 and 125 High Street, Edinburgh 1

Millboard
Jackson's Millboard and Fibre Co. Ltd, Bourne End, Bucks

Handmade and decorative papers
T. N. Lawrence and Sons, 2 Bleeding Heart Yard, Greville Street, London E.C.1

Blocks and finishing tools
T. Mackrell and Co. Ltd, Witham, Essex

Paper and strawboard
Spicer-Cowan Ltd, 19 New Bridge Street, London E.C.4

Gold leaf and foil, handle-letters and brass-type
George M. Whiley Ltd, Victoria Road, South Ruislip, Middlesex

U.S.A.

Equipment and sundries
Craftools Inc, 396 Broadway, New York 13
A. I. Friedman, 25 West 45th Street, New York 36
Ernest Schaefer Co, 74—8 Oraton Street, Newark 4, New Jersey
Technical Library Service, 261 Broadway, New York
Henry Westphal & Co, 4 East 32nd Street, New York

Leather, paper and sundries
Andrews-Nelson-Whitehead Inc, 7 Laight Street, New York 19

Tools and equipment
W. O. Hickok Manufacturing Co, Ninth and Cumberland Streets, Harrisburg, Pennsylvania

Papers
Carter, Rice, Storrs & Bement, 273 Summer Street, Boston, Massachusetts

Bibliography

Works on bookbinding history, design and technique

Bookbinding, Jeff Clements, Arco Publications, London 1963

Bookbinding and the Care of Books, Douglas Cockerell, Pitman, London and New York 1963

The Repairing of Books, Sidney M. Cockerell, Sheppard Press, London 1958

Bookbinding for Beginners, John Corderoy, Studio Vista, London, Watson-Guptill Publications, New York 1967

Bookbinding Then and Now, Lionel Darley, Faber, London 1959

Introduction to Bookbinding, Lionel Darley, Faber, London 1965

Victoria and Albert Museum: Bookbindings, John P. Harthan, HMSO, London 1961

Creative Bookbinding, Pauline Johnson, University of Washington Press, 1965

Basic Bookbinding, A. W. Lewis, Batsford, London 1952, Dover Publications, New York 1957

Modern Design in Bookbinding, Edgar Mansfield, Peter Owen, London 1966 and Boston Books, Boston

Letterpress Bookbinding, John Mason, Pitman, London 1946

Stationery Binding, John Mason, Pitman, London 1946

Edition Case Binding, John Mason, Pitman, London 1946

A History of English Craft Bookbinding Technique, Bernard C. Middleton, Haffner Publishing Company, London and New York 1963

Bookbinding by Hand, Lawrence Town, Faber, London 1951

Modern Bookbinding, Alex J. Vaughan, Charles Skilton, London 1960

Hand Bookbinding: A Manual of Instruction, Aldren A. Watson, Reinhold, New York 1963

Cleaning and Preserving Bindings and Related materials, Carolyn Horton, American Library Association 1967

Index